16

STORIES
THAT SELL
MEMBERSHIPS

GABRIEL ALUISY
With PATRICK FEREDAY

Cover design by Richard Jibaja

ISBN: 978-0-9905832-7-1

10 9 8 7 6 5 4 3 2 1

1. Business & Economics 2. Marketing

First Edition

Published by Shake Creative http://shaketampa.com

Printed in the United States of America

16 STORIES THAT SELL MEMBERSHIPS

SHAKE PRESS

*This book is dedicated to the
#clubchangemakers*

TABLE OF CONTENTS

Introduction

M embership marketing is a tough business. One minute you're on top of the world, the next you are scrambling to make your monthly numbers. There's hardly enough time to celebrate the wins because there's always another fire to put out it seems.

Members age out and retire. Members move. Members pass away. Home prices fall. The economy tanks.

Then, you get another project thrown at you. The newsletter is due. Members pop into your office to complain about last week's event or the latest dress code violation. It's endless.

It's also a rewarding business too.

You get to transform lives. You get to help members make lasting memories. You get to work in a beautiful environment with passionate people. You get to help facilitate meaningful connections.

Like any job, it seems you have to take the good with the bad. That's just part of life.

Or is it?

What if there's a better way?

What if you can change your approach and get drastically different results? What if instead of scrambling each month to hit your goals, you've got a full membership, and even a waiting list to join?

With that stress off your plate, you'd be free to tackle the other tasks your job requires. And those wouldn't seem so tough anymore.

In this book, we'll show you how to do just that. We'll show you how to turn your "ads" into "stories." We'll show you how to make those stories so compelling that prospects are asking - no, actually begging - to join your club.

We'll also show you how your follow-ups can be automated. No more sticky notes or spreadsheets to keep track of emails and calls you need to make, you've got that handled automatically.

Finally, as a bonus, we'll share a few time-saving tips like how to answer your prospects frequently asked questions automatically or how to let them book tours without emailing you. If all of that sounds good, buckle up and read on!

WHY STORIES?

We opt to use the term "story" over the term "ad" for a crucial reason: With stories, you're not "selling" a membership, you're creating an opportunity. As a membership professional, this should always be your goal.

The other reason we use this term is that marketing is often confused with advertising. We think if you market right, you'll never have to advertise.

Clubs with a 501(c)7 designation cannot advertise, but they can market. We think that storytelling helps to define that difference.

HOW TO READ THIS BOOK

This book is meant to be a springboard for ideas. We'll provide 16 examples of stories you can use to better inform potential prospects about why your club is right for them.

Are there more than 16? Sure. Our goal is to get you thinking creatively. So consider this a starting point. If you come up with more stories, we'd love to hear them!

Some of these stories will work for you and some won't depending on your club's circumstances. That's OK too. Every club is different so take what you can use and ignore what you can't. You won't hurt our feelings, we promise.

WHAT THIS BOOK IS AND IS NOT

This book IS going to give you many ideas and get you thinking about telling your club's story in a new way. It's also going to give you

This book is NOT going to give you a step by step action plan. I wrote another book a couple of years ago, *The Definitive Guide to Membership Marketing*, that will give you specific steps you can take to deliver your stories in an effective way. Consider this a great compliment to that book.

WHY WE USED FACEBOOK EXAMPLES

Throughout the book, we used examples of *actual* Facebook campaigns we ran for our clients that performed well. These stories generated thousands of membership leads that turned into millions of dollars in revenue for our clients. It's one of the things we do best at the Private Club Agency.

However, these story types are in no way limited to Facebook campaigns. They will work well as email blasts, on other social networks like LinkedIn or Instagram, in videos, on mailers and all sorts of other mediums too.

For consistency, we just chose to pick one.

Cold, Warm & Hot Prospects

There are many different types of stories that can be effectively used. Some stories compel your prospects to take action, like download a brochure or schedule a tour. Others simply set a tone with no call to action at all.

You've heard the term, "timing is everything," and as cliché as that phrase has become, it's true. Telling the right type of story at the right time is the first key to success.

So understanding your prospect's life-cycle is a key component to crafting an effective membership campaign.

Before actually becoming members, all prospects will progress through the following life-cycle phases: Unaware Prospect, Aware Prospect and Interested Prospect.

It may be easier to think of them as Cold, Warm and Hot prospects.

Cold prospects are those who don't even know your club is there. They may be new to the area for instance. Maybe they're not golfers or maybe they just don't get out much.

Warm prospects know about the club. These folks may not have a complete picture, but they are relatively aware you exist and what you can offer.

Hot prospects are ones that are truly considering membership. They have been to your website, been a guest of a member or have otherwise interacted with your stories in the past. They are right on the edge and, with the right story, they're likely to join.

Throughout this book you'll see which story types work best for each of these stages. There's also one other key ingredient you need to recognize...

Quantity
vs.
Quality

Some stories you tell will be attractive to a large quantity of people. Other stories are only meant for a select group.

If you've been in a marketing role, you've probably heard the term "funnel" before. While it may sound like a difficult concept, it's actually pretty straightforward.

What a funnel does is it takes a large quantity of cold prospects and filters them down to a smaller quantity of hot prospects.

In other words, we cast a wider net at the top, and as our prospects progress through the life-cycle stages, we have a narrower set of targeting toward the bottom.

Funnels are usually represented by a graphic like this (see next page).

Our stories will act similarly. In the beginning of any membership campaign, we'll want to tell our stories to as many qualified folks as possible. Our subsequent messages will further narrow them down until we find our ideal membership candidates. We start with quantity and end with quality.

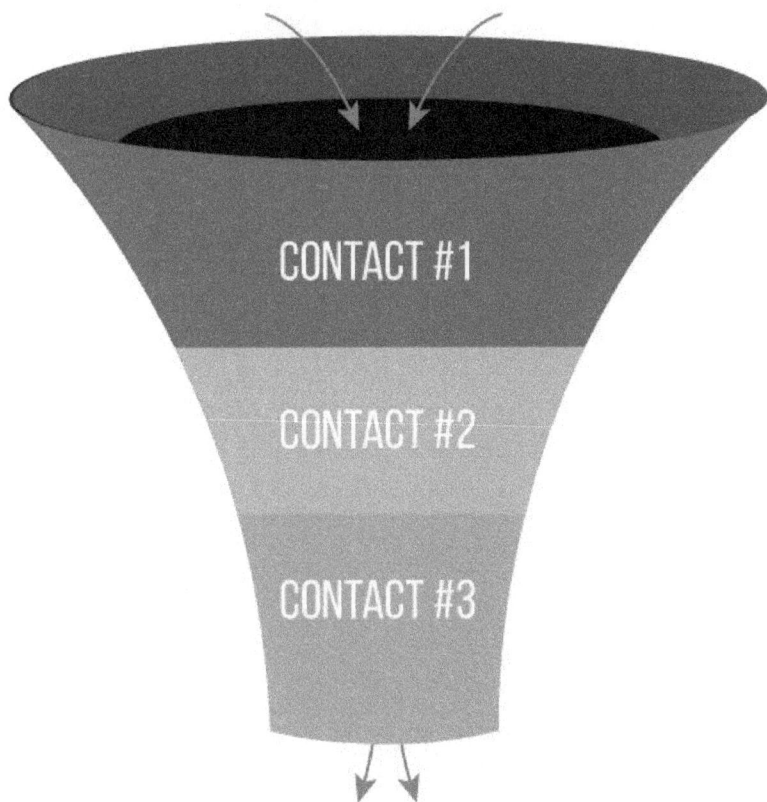

PROSPECTS

CONTACT #1

CONTACT #2

CONTACT #3

MEMBERS

The Story Matrix

A t The Private Club Agency, we created a methodology to help our clients tell their stories to the right audience at the right time. We developed a strategy to move a large quantity of cold prospects into a smaller group of hot prospects.

We chose 16 different story structures in order to do this. Each story was graphed along a time-line (figure 2 on the next page).

On the vertical axis we have Quantity to Quality. Along the horizontal axis we have Cold to Warm. Very simply we want to create a membership prospect journey that starts in the top left of the matrix and moves people into the bottom right side of the matrix.

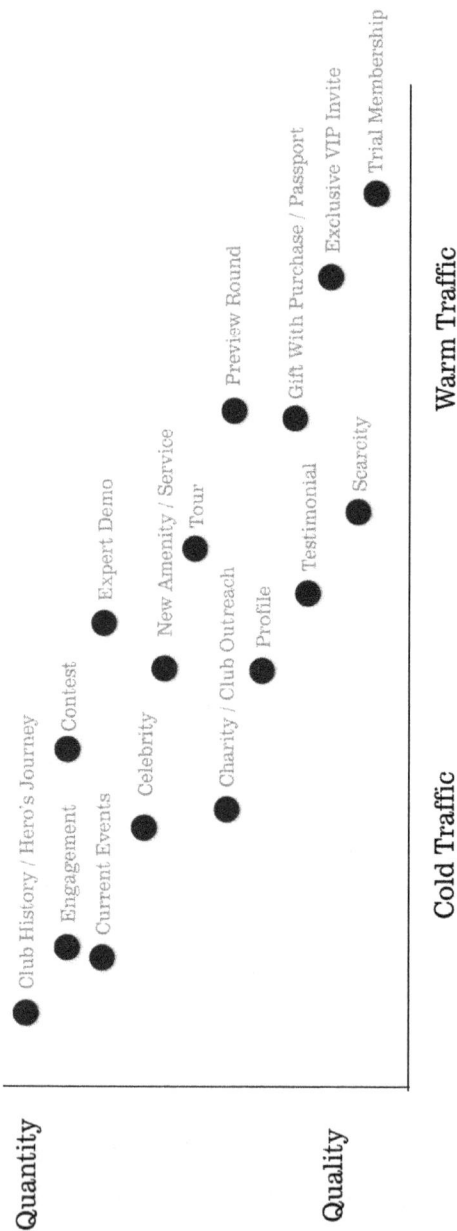

Quantity

Quality

Club History / Hero's Journey

Engagement

Current Events

Contest

Celebrity

Expert Demo

New Amenity / Service Tour

Charity / Club Outreach

Profile

Preview Round

Testimonial

Scarcity

Gift With Purchase / Passport

Exclusive VIP Invite

Trial Membership

Cold Traffic

Warm Traffic

As you can see, stories like the Hero's Journey or Current Events are meant for a large quantity of colder prospects while stories like the Testimonial or the Preview Membership are meant for a much smaller audience of warmer prospects.

The stories toward the top left of the matrix have no calls to action while the stories in the bottom right side are filled with very specific calls to action. We want our warmest prospects to experience the club in person by taking a tour, playing a preview round or attending an event.

Blasting out the same message to everyone is a mistake that many membership marketing folks make. Don't let that be you.

Ideally, when you're running a campaign, it's best to have some of your stories targeted at the larger quantity cold audiences, some at the smaller warmer audiences and some in between. By doing so, you'll keep a constant flow of traffic in your funnel. We want a good number of people at every stage.

In the following pages, we'll show you the power of these sixteen story arcs and we'll provide a template you can use at your club or business.

We hope you'll enjoy them and maybe they'll even spark some ideas of your own.

Story #1
Club History /
Hero's Journey

ESSENTIAL INFORMATION

- Can you tell an interesting story that appeals to a wide audience?
- Can you build some drama or suspense?
- Can you show the passion & dedication of the members and staff?
- This could be the first interaction for many people

HOW IT WORKS

What's your club's compelling why? What struggle did the founding members go through to build your club? What is the level of dedication your staff brings to the members? These are all topics you can use to tell your club's story.

The heroes journey is a great story structure to use. It includes a main protagonist (your founding members), a goal to achieve (why we should root for you), a challenge to overcome and a happy ending. Remember, the challenge is the crucial part that will engage your audience.

Lochmoor Club ✔
Written by Gabriel Aluisy [?] · Just now · 🌐

👍 **Like Page**   •••

Lochmoor Club was founded in 1917 when a group of Detroit golf enthusiasts bought 135 acres of flat farm land not far from Lake St. Clair. Travis Beaupre and Sweeney Walter Travis, three-time U.S. Amateur Golf Champion helped design the original course, and it was built by John H. Sweeney.

The original clubhouse was just a farmhouse on the property which burnt to the ground in 1924, and on that very same day, the directors of the club met and approved construction of a new clubhouse. In 1965 after inspection, the foundations of this rebuilt clubhouse were deemed unfit, so a demolition occurred and the clubhouse you see today was built and still stands proud.

Upon the opening of this clubhouse on Thanksgiving Day, 1969 further improvements to the club were made. Tennis courts were built, an irrigation system installed, and over 2,000 trees and shrubs planted to beautify the property. A fascinating transformation from 1917 to today occurred on this property, and for a more detailed timeline of events visit the history page of our website.

LOCHMOOR.CLUBMEMBERSHIP.INFO
A Fascinating History of The Iconic Lochmoor Club

Learn More

Story #2
New Amenity or Service

ESSENTIAL INFORMATION

- What is the new 'thing?'
- What are the benefits to members?
- Consider including the price of construction and opening date
- Do you want to give tours?

HOW IT WORKS

Humans love progress. We're always looking to go further, fly higher and break records. So we love to hear stories about others improving and refining. We love to hear about new features or amenities being added. So don't be shy to showcase what you're doing.

We tell our clients to mimic what Disney does when they release a new ride. They leak blue prints and renderings, they show photos of the progress being made, they play video clips of what it will look like when it's ready and they give select audiences a sneak peak.

Boca Lago Country Club
Sponsored · 🌐

Fueled by a comprehensive multi-million-dollar renovation project that has enhanced all aspects of the membership experience, a new era is officially underway at Boca Lago Country Club and we want your family to be a part of it all!

Now offering traveling membership benefits at 300+ clubs nationwide, there's never been a better time to experience all Boca Lago has to offer.

BOCALAGOCOUNTRY.CLUBMEMBERSHIP.INFO
Be Part of a New Era at Boca Lago Country Club   Learn More
Come experience the new Boca Lago Country Club...

Story #3
Testimonial

ESSENTIAL INFORMATION

- Highlight benefits of the club
- Community, quality, staff attention, memories, friendships are all good subjects
- Ensure length of their membership is stated
- Emphasis is more on 'feelings' than 'great golf or stunning amenities.

HOW IT WORKS

It's one thing for you to tell a story, but it's a lot more powerful if someone tells a story *about* you. We call this "social proof" and it's one of the most valuable stories out there.

Gathering testimonials should be strategic. They don't need to be long, in fact just a few short sentences works, but they need to speak to real issues that your potential members might have - providing a safe and secure environment, making business connections, forming friendships and having a place to relax and play. Getting testimonials where members state how the club makes them "feel" is where the gold is.

Lochmoor Club
Sponsored · 🌐

Come take a tour of Lochmoor Club's historic clubhouse and facilities today.

Our golf course is set to return to pristine conditions this year. For a limited time you can schedule a visit with us to learn about all the improvements we're making to the club.

"For the 40 years we've been members, Lochmoor has enriched our lives. It's the place our children learned to play golf and tennis and it's where we have had the best of times with the best of friends." - Dave Z.

LOCHMOOR.CLUBMEMBERSHIP.INFO
Tour Lochmoor Club Today   Learn More
Relax, Golf, Play, Live

Story #4
Expert Demo

ESSENTIAL INFORMATION

- Typically a video is best here
- Enlist your golf pros, tennis pros, chef, bartender and other club staff
- Can it interest viewers for 30 seconds plus?
- Does it also represent the club?

HOW IT WORKS

Teaching your prospects a skill is a great way to show-case the club *and* provide value. Remember, people don't like to be "sold" to, so always strive to add value first.

The law of reciprocity is a real thing. When you give someone a gift, most feel an obligation to repay that favor in some way. Even if it's just simply sharing with a friend.

Video works best for this type of story. Over the years, we've encouraged our clients to shoot videos of their pro demoing a swing tip, their chef sharing a recipe se-cret or their bartender mixing up a cocktail.

Spring Meadows Country Club
Sponsored · 🌐

Ever wondered what the pros are doing with computers on the range?

Our head pro talks you through the Trackman software and how it can benefit you. The measurements you can receive from this system will change the way you think of the golf swing. Watch the tutorial and learn about our new Trackman golf lessons.

SPRINGMEADOWS.CLUBMEMBERSHIP.INFO
Learn About Our New Trackman Lessons

Join as a Golf Member in September or October No du…

Learn More

Story #5
Celebrity

ESSENTIAL INFORMATION

- Does your club have a famous member?
- Are there tournaments played at your club?
- Any images of celebrities at your club?
- Can you get a testimonial from them?

HOW IT WORKS

Celebrity sells. Plain and simple. Whether they stopped by for a round or a meal, make sure to grab a photo (with their permission of course) and ask them what they thought of your club - use that as a quote.

Do make sure to have them sign a release allowing you to use their image and do honor their privacy if they wish to remain discreet of course.

If you've hosted a tournament past or present, make sure to tell the story of the preparation that's involved, showcase the winner, any records that were broken or anything else that defined the event.

Inwood Country Club
Sponsored · ⚙

Inwood played host to the 1921 PGA Championship, won by Walter Hagen, and the 1923 U.S. Open Championship, scene of Bobby Jones' victory and famous "shot heard 'round the world". Today, visitors to Inwood will see noteworthy memorabilia which evoke the excitement and drama of those events.

Click below to learn more about the club, and discover unique membership opportunities.

INWOODCOUNTRY.CLUBMEMBERSHIP.INFO
Did You Know Inwood Has Hosted Two Major Championships?

Learn More

Story #6
Charity

ESSENTIAL INFORMATION

- Try to change 'snooty' perception
- What do you do for the community?
- How long have you helped locally?
- Why do you do this, what do you enjoy helping?
- Trying to win heart and minds

HOW IT WORKS

Private clubs, luxury resorts and other high end brands often get a bad rap. They're characterized as playgrounds for rich elitists who do nothing for the community. It's simply not true!

The National Golf Foundation measures the charitable impact of golf at $3.9 Billion per year! Clubs are actually giving back in a big way - through jobs, charitable contributions and volunteer efforts.

Your club is doing something. If you're not directly, your members are. This is a powerful story to tell. Get pictures of the big checks they hand out. Tell the story of why your club cares about a specific cause. Showcase members and staff who donate their time and money.

Lochmoor Club
Sponsored · 🌐

Lochmoor is so proud of the efforts its members make in helping out the local community. Every year we host the Lochmoor fights Cancer Golf Outing, where all funds raised go to the Van Elslander cancer center. A great day is had by everyone involved and together we are helping fight a greater cause. So proud of this wonderful community. #appreciationpost

LOCHMOOR.CLUBMEMBERSHIP.INFO
Lochmoor Raises $30,000 In The Fight Against Cancer
Our members had another successful outing this year raising money to...

Story #7
Current Events

ESSENTIAL INFORMATION

- Tied to an event - The Masters, July 4th, etc.
- Relate the current event to your club
- Encouraging likes/shares/comments is a bonus

HOW IT WORKS

Fun attracts people. You can use the energy from your events to show why your club is a hub of activity. One of the best times to do this is when there is a national or international event taking place.

Does your club have any traditions for Derby Day? Do you roll out a red carpet for the Oscars? Build on the buzz that surrounds these events by attaching your club's brand to it.

Burlington Country Club
Sponsored · 🌐

It's almost time for the Derby!

Last year we had a great celebration so this year we are doing the same. On Derby weekend come and enjoy snacks and drinks from the bar, then move onto the grill room for the main event. This year we have some limited guest passes. You don't want to miss the Derby at Burlington

DISPLAYURL.COM

Come and Join Us For Our Annual Kentucky Derby Party

Learn More

Story #8
Engagement

ESSENTIAL INFORMATION

- This should cater to a wide audience
- Video is an option here
- Do you want shares/likes/comments/views?
- Typically you should ask a question
- Is it a compelling post?
- Users that engage can be re-targeted

HOW IT WORKS

People love to give their opinions. This type of story allows them to do that. It puts them in the moment and encourages engagement. Get creative and ask a compelling question like, "what club would you hit here," or "what's your favorite summertime snack?" Just make sure that it goes along with something the club is doing.

When this is done on social media, posts get more traction because platforms love when users like, comment and share which they'll do in spades with these.

The Suburban Club
Sponsored · ◷

What club are you hitting in?

Our longest hole is the par five 9th, playing 554 yards from the tips. Who thinks they could get home in two, and what clubs are you hitting?

For a limited time new members receive three months of complimentary dues. Learn about the Club and find out more by clicking below.

HOLE	1	2	3	4	5	6	7	8	9	Out		10	11	12	13	14	15	16	17	18	In	Tot	
BLUE	386	175	405	426	424	168	370	394	554	3305		395	407	494	204	396	433	150	418	340	3237	6542	
WHITE	365	168	376	394	411	155	363	370	536	3118		382	373	480	198	392	404	138	403	334	3108	6226	
GREEN	350	150	345	365	399	136	332	340	453	2863		321	355	432	182	346	380	126	390	328	2850	5712	
HANDICAP	11	15	7	3	1	17	13	9	5			8	10	4	16	12	2	18	6	14			
PAR	4	3	4	4	4	3	4	4	5	35		4	4	5	3	4	4	3	4	4	35	70	
RED	318	136	332	315	404	122	325	335	448	2755		315	350	400	172	310	401	116	364	322	2750	5505	
HANDICAP	11	15	7	1	5	17	13	9	3			10	4	2	16	12	8	18	6	14			
PAR	4	3	4	4	5	3	4	4	5	36		4	4	5	3	4	5	3	4	4	36	72	

DATE: _____

SCORER: _____

ATTEST: _____

All yardages measured to middle of green.

USGA	Course Rating	Slope Rating
Blue	72.3	129
White	71.0	127
Green – M	69.0	124
Green – W	73.0	133
Red	72.0	130

Story #9
Contest

ESSENTIAL INFORMATION

- What can you offer as a prize?
- Is there a deadline for entry?
- How many prizes are available?
- Tie the contest into something special your club offers.

HOW IT WORKS

The lottery exists for a reason. People love to play games and win prizes.

What does your club offer that's second to none? Tie it into a contest if you can.

It might just be the nudge your warmer prospect needs to get them to take a tour or schedule a visit.

Looking to improve your game?

There's no better place than Tampa Country Club to do it.

Our talented staff of PGA professionals is ready to tune your game and get you into the single digits.

Take a tour this month and get entered into our drawing for a year's worth of professional lessons when you join.

Raise Your Game With Golf Lessons For An Entire Year

Learn More

SIXTEEN STORIES THAT SELL MEMBERSHIPS

Story #10
Mixer or
VIP Invite

ESSENTIAL INFORMATION

- What does the applicant get?
- Can you create a prospect event?
- Use urgency by limiting the availability
- Use urgency by creating a deadline
- How do you qualify applicants?

HOW IT WORKS

As we get into the warmer prospects, the ones that have shown some interest, it's time to try to get them to the club. It's important for them to experience it firsthand. A prospective member mixer or similar VIP event is one way to do that.

Please note: the statement, "Request your invitation," is an important one. It limits your downside exposure and allows you to say no to folks you don't believe are qualified.

The Players
Sponsored · ⚙

Come experience an evening at Manhattan's friendliest private social club at one of our September mixers. Enjoy beer & wine as well as a tour of our historic clubhouse. Only 25 invites are available so request your VIP invitation now.

THEPLAYERS.CLUBMEMBERSHIP.INFO
Be Our Guest   Learn More
Hurry, only 25 invites available!

Story #11
Scarcity

ESSENTIAL INFORMATION

- What is the scarce offer?
- How many are available?
- Is there a time limit/restriction?
- What will people lose by not acting?

HOW IT WORKS

Scarcity taps into our primordial survival instincts. It's an effective way to get people to stop hemming and hawing and to take action.

By limiting your offer to a certain time or a certain quantity, you also lift the reputation and esteem of your club.

Use this type of story for warmer audiences that need that final push.

Briar Ridge Country Club
Sponsored · 🌐

Looking for Northwest Indiana's best Private Club?

For a limited time Briar Ridge is offering one day VIP member passes to qualified individuals. Come and enjoy spectacular golf, tennis, and dining options and see why Briar Ridge is the region's outstanding Club.

BRIARRIDGE.CLUBMEMBERSHIP.INFO
Be A Member For The Day
Only 25 VIP passes are available!

[Learn More]

Story #12
Preview Round

ESSENTIAL INFORMATION

- What is included in offer?
- Urgency – how many are available?
- When is the Deadline?
- How do you qualify applicant?

HOW IT WORKS

As we get into the warmer prospects, the ones that have shown some interest, it's time to try to get them to the club. It's important for them to experience it firsthand.

A preview round of golf is one way to do that. Talk is cheap, so let them experience your exceptional course conditions, pace of play and friendly staff in person.

When combined with the scarce offer, it's even more effective.

For a limited time, The Club at Olde Cypress is offering the chance to become a member for a day - including a VIP Tour, lunch and round of golf on our PB Dye Championship Course

Hurry, this offer is limited to the first 10.

OLDECYPRESS.CLUBMEMBERSHIP.INFO
Experience the Club at Olde Cypress   Request Time
Hurry, offer limited to first 10

Story #13
Tour

ESSENTIAL INFORMATION

- Try to get new prospects on site
- Highlight some key benefits of club
- Is there a limit, sense of urgency?
- Does tour include lunch, drink etc?

HOW IT WORKS

While not as impressive as a preview round or VIP mixer, the tour can be just as effective.

If you've properly told the New Amenity or Service story to a colder audience, this will work perfectly. Folks will want to see firsthand the improvements you've made.

Some things to highlight include: what folks can expect from this tour, how long it will last and how many are available.

The Forest Country Club
Sponsored · 🌐

With renovations now complete, our brand new clubhouse is the most impressive in the Ft. Myers area. Complete with indoor and outdoor dining options, fire pits, fitness facilities, and glorious golf views.

As part of our 40th anniversary celebrations we invite you to come and experience it for yourself. Tours are limited to the first ten applicants so schedule your visit today.

THEFORESTCOUNTRY.CLUBMEMBERSHIP.INFO

Take a Tour of Our Brand New Clubhouse   Learn More

Tours are limited to the first 10 qualified applicants!

Story #14
Trial Membership

ESSENTIAL INFORMATION

- What does the trial entail?
- Duration of trial?
- Do fees contribute to initiation fee?
- Are numbers limited?

HOW IT WORKS

It's time to move them from warm to hot. Let them experience the story of your club for themselves for an extended period of time.

Many clubs offer a trial or seasonal membership to get their prospects acclimated to the club before joining as full members.

If you do, we'd suggest limiting this membership to no more than 3 months. They need to have skin in the game to stick around, so we'd also suggest having them pay full dues and potentially a small initiation fee that would roll into full membership fees.

During the time of their trial membership, it's important to be in touch with them weekly to keep a continual gauge of how things are progressing.

The Club at Hammock Beach Resort
Sponsored · 🌐

Introducing our 30 Day Preview Membership!

Experience unlimited surf, sun, golf & tennis at Palm Coast's premier resort club for an entire month!

HURRY, this offer is limited to the first 25 new members.

Schedule your VIP club tour today!

HAMMOCKBEACHMEMBERSHIP.COM

30 Day Preview Memberships Available

30-day Preview Membership Experience unlimited surf,...

Apply Now

Story #15
Gift With
Purchase

ESSENTIAL INFORMATION

- New members receive a gift
- Passport option – bonuses every month
- Create additional value to prospects

HOW IT WORKS

We hate discounting. But if you feel there needs to be value added to the equation we'd instead suggest a "gift with a purchase."

Over the years, we've used a club passport as a way to do that. The reason it works is because new members get to experience many different parts of the club and there is an offer that keeps them coming back month after month. As a result, retention rates rise.

It's also a better incentive for referring members than a discount off of dues. Guard your dues line at all costs. The true cost of these offers is low if not completely offset by the member spend that will result from them redeeming it.

The Suburban Club
Sponsored · ⊕

Introducing our passport program! Treats for every month of the year.

As a token of appreciation, all new members will receive our new passport compromising of all sorts of wonderful treats. Gifts range from dining vouchers, to golf lessons, to bottles of wine. Find out the full schedule of passport treats, and schedule your visit today.

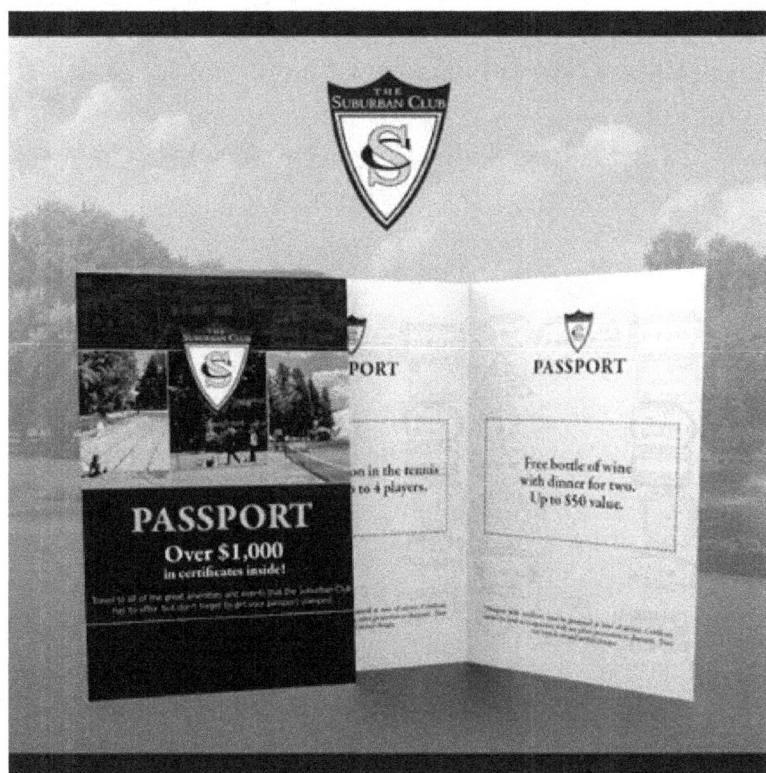

SUBURBAN.CLUBMEMBERSHIP.INFO

Join Suburban and Receive Our New Passport Program as a Gift To You

Learn More

Story #16
Profile

ESSENTIAL INFORMATION

- Highlight a personal story of a member or staff member
- Showcase their dedication to the mission, vision and core values of your organization

HOW IT WORKS

The club and resort business is a people business and in the end it's the people that make the experience magical. So make sure to put your people front and center.

You can combine this story with the hero's journey for an extra powerful result.

If you can tie their personal story into the club's mission, vision and/or core values you've got a home run.

Private Club Agency
Just now · 🌐

Our employee of the month for April is Richard, our head designer. He moved to the US from Ecuador in 2016 and has been with us ever since. His background in design and artwork is extensive and he even taught design classes before moving here.

Richard works on an array of client projects from websites, to brochures, banners, and packaging. Clients love his work and are always involved with the creative process. He really enjoys bringing a clients ideas to life, and he learns every day from their feedback on his creations.

Richard is a key figure in The Private Club Agency and we are grateful for all the hard work he contributes. Congraulations Richard

PRIVATECLUBAGENCY.COM
August Employee of The Month   Learn More
Richard is our head designer and one of the most...

Great Story, Now What?

Now that you've gotten really great at telling stories, you should have a plan in place to get your prospects to take action. This most often means filling out a form with their name, telephone and email at a bare minimum.

Many folks make the mistake of sending their prospects directly to their website. The problem with that is there's generally too much information and no clear action to take. Before the prospect finds it, they've gotten distracted by kids, dogs, work, etc. and clicked away or logged off their device.

It's important that your stories lead to a landing page built specifically for the campaign. It should speak to the same story you told in the first place.

There should be a clear way to provide their personal information up at the top of the page, not buried in the middle or the bottom.

The page should include photos, testimonials and specific information about your club such as the facilities and amenities it offers. It's important to provide the basics, but don't overwhelm people with too much detail.

Very importantly there should be no links on the page. There should be no way for them to click elsewhere except to fill out that form. When you remove all distractions, you'll have a better chance of getting them to take action and fill in their details.

Here are a few examples of landing pages that have been effective at generating prospects for our clients:

CITY CLUB EXAMPLE:
https://theplayers.clubmembership.info
(see screenshot on facing page)

GOLF CLUB EXAMPLE:
http://jacksonvillecountry.clubmembership.info

BEACH CLUB EXAMPLE:
http://serenatabeachclub.com

Here is an actual landing page we built for The Players. It's so long that it takes 2 pages in this book. It gives the visitor just enough info without being overwhelming.

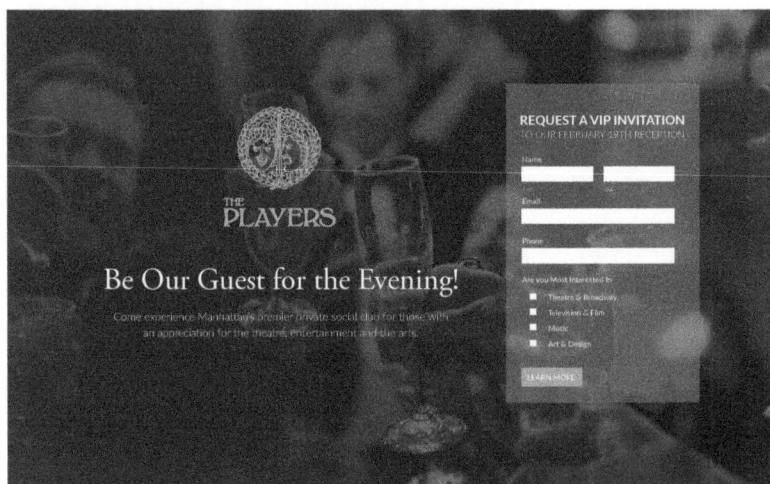

About Our Membership

The Players is a private social club that draws its membership from the theatre community and the related fields of film, television, music and publishing, as well as arts lovers from a broad range of professions. What makes The Players unlike any other club is our spirit of fun and camaraderie. Performer or patron, civilian or celebrity, we all have a great time together.

A Few Reasons to Consider Membership at The Players

For fun
Day or night, there's always a reason to drop by The Players. From lonely performances to a late night out with friends after work, The Players is always your home away from home.

For travelers
Enjoy access to exclusive reciprocal & arts worldwide including The Garrick Club in London, The Cosmos Club in Washington D.C. and The Magic Castle in Los Angeles.

For readers
The Library at The Players is a literary lover's dream, a festive and elegant setting with a world-class collection of classic theatre publications and books.

For art lovers
We house a remarkable art collection featuring work by John Singer Sargent, Everett Raymond Kinstler, Al Hirschfeld and many more.

More than 130 years later, the tradition continues.

Here is an actual landing page we built for Jacksonville Golf & Country Club. As you'll see it's a similar setup.

Jacksonville
GOLF & COUNTRY CLUB
Established 1989

Join now before prices go up!

Pay social dues and get Full Membership Access during a Trial Membership. Golf/Full members have access to 22 area golf courses this summer!

Request Your VIP Guest Pass

Name

First   Last

Email

Phone

HURRY,
This offer is limited to the first 25 new members.

Here's what people are saying about
Jacksonville Golf & Country Club

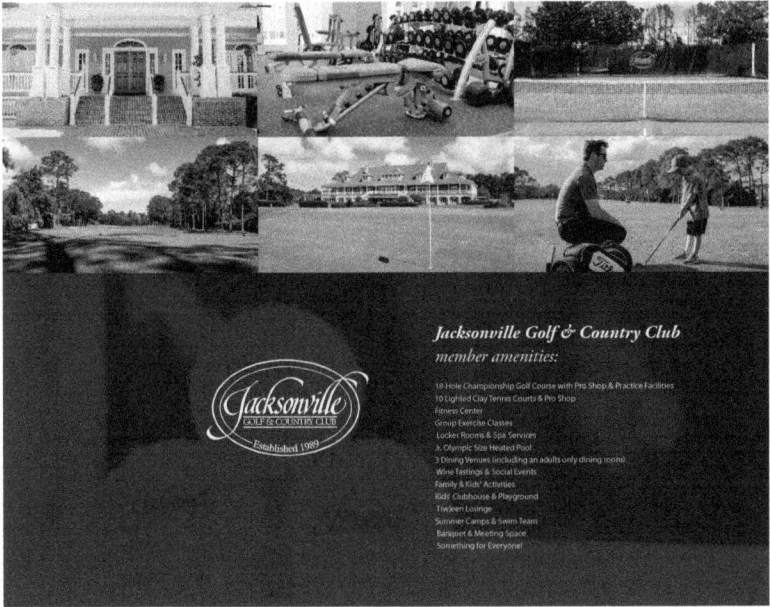

About
Jacksonville Golf & Country Club

Jacksonville Golf & Country Club, a controlled access community and private member-owned club, was an Arvida project that saw its first residents move in during the fall of 1989. The Club opened and the first round of golf was played on the course in November of that same year. In April of 1998, the Club turned over from Arvida's ownership and management to the Club membership. The equity membership allows club members to purchase a share of the ownership of the club and its operations through the purchase of their home/property in Jacksonville Golf & Country Club. Non-equity memberships are also available in limited numbers and do not include a community property purchase. Currently we have just under 800 members, and we hope to add you to our membership!

3985 Hunt Club Road, Jacksonville, FL 32224

Again, just as much info as needed. No links. No place to get sidetracked. We want the visitor to fill out the form and nothing else.

Once we have the membership leads, the next step is... you guessed it - continuing to tell the club's story. We prefer to do that with automation.

Automation

When you get really good at telling your story, your club's membership funnel begins to fill. On average, our agency's clients generate 30 - 60 qualified leads per month. So by month three, there could be anywhere from 90 to 180 prospects at various stages of their funnel. That's when automation becomes crucial.

If you're still using an old fashioned spreadsheet, sticky notes, a day planner or similar, it's time to get more sophisticated. There are great software platforms out there to keep track of your prospects and the communication you've had with them. In addition to club-specific systems, tools like HubSpot and MailChimp offer low cost or no cost ways to automatically keep track and follow up with your prospects.

Once you begin running campaigns you'll find your prospects will reach out at very odd hours of the day. The vast majority of our client's leads come in between the hours of 6am and 9am and from 7pm - 9pm. The chart below shows actual web traffic times from one of our campaigns. This is a very typical distribution.

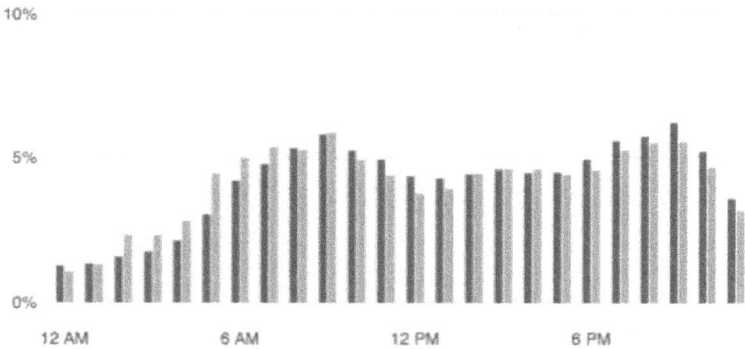

When you think about it, it makes sense. Most people will be reading your stories before and after they go to work. Especially if they're reading them on a social media platform like Facebook, Instagram or LinkedIn.

Hopefully you're not working at 6am or 9pm too often. Even for the club business that's pretty extreme. But in today's world, people expect immediate gratification. They want a quick answer to a question or they want to book a time for their tour on the spot.

If you don't have automation in place, you'll run the risk of losing their interest - especially those on the colder side of the matrix.

At a bare minimum, you need to have an automatic email go out right when the form is completed. Better still, we'd recommend an automated series of emails that drip out over a number of weeks or months.

It takes between 5 - 12 touches at a minimum for a member to join your club. For this reason, we like to build our clients a 12 week automated email series. Now there's no need to stress out about follow-ups.

By the way, you don't have to re-invent the wheel with your emails. Use the stories we highlighted above as starting points for your email communication with membership prospects.

The other great thing about our email series is that we can identify the warmer and hotter prospects by their email opens and clicks. This data is provided by all decent email systems and helps us recognize who might need a text, call or further contact.

AUTOMATED SCHEDULING

Another way to save valuable time is to automate the process of scheduling visits and tours to the club. We recommend tools like Calendly and YouCanBookMe so that membership prospects can choose from an available list of times on your calender.

Instead of 3 to 5 emails back and forth to confirm a tour time, our client's prospects have this task automated saving them as much as 15 minutes of work per prospect. When you've got 30 - 60 prospects in your funnel each month, this can really add up quick!

With these tools and the proper setup, you can link directly to your Gmail or Outlook calendar and choose your available days and times each week. There is a two way link, so when you have an appointment booked on your calendar it automatically blocks that time off the booking page to prevent double-bookings. It's magic.

If you want to check out one of these in action, simply visit https://privateclubagency.com/meet.

Choosing the Right Partner

Many clubs do not have the infrastructure to be able to take on the full burden of a membership marketing campaign. There's a lot involved from choosing the right story to setting up the demographic targeting, and from building the landing page and automation to generating monthly reporting and analyzing the key metrics.

Sometimes it's best to hire a partner that can help to guide decision making and help execute the tasks associated with the campaign. Luckily a few great specialized firms exist within the private club industry. In this final section of the book, we'll show you how to choose the right partner if you need some help along the way.

INDUSTRY EXPERIENCE

First and foremost, it's important to find a partner that is experienced in the nuances of the private club industry. Specialized firms are able to provide guidance on what can and cannot be said in your stories to protect your non-profit status.

Just as importantly, they'll help you navigate the many layers of club governance in order to get full buy-in from the board. As you know, that can be a full-time job in itself.

Generally speaking, your local marketing firm is just not going to be well versed enough to understand the intricacies of your governance structure, membership categories or supply useful benchmarks for your club. They're also not going to be able to talk the board's language most times.

ROI AND RESULTS

In order to determine how effective an agency is, there are some key metrics that you should consider. Many of these are detailed in the book, *The Definitive Guide to Membership Marketing*, but the main ones include cost per click, cost per conversion (what it costs on average to generate a lead) and return on investment (ROI).

When considering an agency partner, ask them to provide you these key performance indicators (KPIs).

It's best to find current benchmarks on these KPIs. This can be easily accomplished with a web search. Keep in mind that this data is platform independent (Google Adwords, Facebook Ads, LinkedIn Ads, will all have different benchmarks) so just make sure to compare apples to apples.

For instance, as of 2019, the average cost per lead on the Facebook platform is around $19. Make sure that your partner can beat that considerably and compare that against other firms you are considering.

FEE STRUCTURE

There are different ways that your agency partner can work with you and fees can be dramatically different from agency to agency. Some partners will charge set-up fees as well as a monthly fee, while others may only charge a monthly fee.

In some cases, an agency may work on a commission-only basis. In this structure, you pay only for performance. You might pay per lead or a commission on a new member. This limits your downside risk significantly.

Our own agency has done this with specific clubs who we felt were in the right market and had the right mix of amenities and services. It's a no-cost way to get started! Don't be afraid to ask an agency if that option is available to you.

MARKET PENETRATION

One last very important thing to consider when choosing a partner is their market penetration. In other words, how many clubs are they currently working with in your city or market?

The only answer they should give is zero.

Why? Because if they are working with multiple clubs in the same market then they are cannibalizing potential membership prospects. If they work with one other club they are only sending 1/2 of the prospects to you. If they already work with two clubs, they are only sending you 1/3. On it goes.

The only exception involves clubs of a completely different type. In major cities we might work with one city club, one golf club and one yacht club for instance. So just make sure there is some type of non-compete clause in place.

Action Time

Now that you've read this book, you're hopefully full of ideas. While ideas are great, they're not valuable in and of themselves. So please make sure to put this book into action.

There's nothing worse than wasted knowledge. Don't read it and put it back on your shelf. Make sure to take a copy into your next membership committee meeting, managers meeting or chapter meeting and discuss which stories you want to begin telling. Devise a plan to get your stories out and utilize a partner if you need some help. Just don't wait to take action. We trust if you made it this far you will, and as we say around our office...

Here's to your membership success!

About the Author

GABRIEL ALUISY is the private club industry's best-selling author. His latest books include *The Definitive Guide to Membership Marketing* and *The ABC's of Plutonium Private Club Leadership* which he co-authored with Michael Crandal, CNG.

He hosts the longest running, most listened-to weekly podcast, *The Private Club Radio Show*.

As President of The Private Club Agency, he has worked with and educated hundreds of club leaders around the world.

He enjoys connecting with club leaders just like you so feel free to reach out to him with any questions or challenges you might have.

YOU CAN EMAIL HIM DIRECTLY AT:
gabe@privateclubagency.com

About the Featured Contributor

PATRICK FEREDAY is a marketing executive and strategist at The Private Club Agency. He earned his MBA in Business Analytics from the University of Tampa and has previously worked for the Professional Golfer's Association of Europe. He manages the marketing campaigns of private clubs around the country.

About The Private Club Agency

WHO WE ARE:

Our staff is comprised of a dedicated team of designers, social media experts, copywriters and marketers who share a passion for telling remarkable stories and creating eye-catching visuals.

We've won a number of awards for graphic design and branding, but we're more proud of the fact that we've helped drive millions of dollars of membership revenue to clubs around the country.

WHAT WE DO:

We solve the 3 major problems facing private clubs:

1. Aging Membership – we help clubs stay relevant and attract younger members.

2. Historical Gender Gaps – we help clubs become a haven for the whole family.

3. Competition for Entertainment Dollars – we help clubs raise brand value and become sought after destinations.

Our team has worked with private clubs across the country to drive membership sales and increase membership retention. We do this by combining award winning graphic design with targeted marketing strategies while offering our clients guidance and advice.

HOW WE WORK:

We take on a limited number of clients each season. This ensures we can provide our clients with the full attention and care they deserve.

We only work with one club per market.

THE
P**RIVATE**CL UB
A G E N C Y

Want to Work With Us?

Please email team@privateclubagency.com to setup a complimentary consultation.

Other Books by Gabriel Aluisy

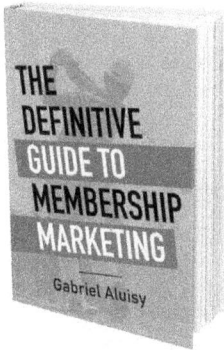

The Definitive Guide to Membership Marketing

This book is the missing guide they never handed you when you took that role as general manager, membership director or membership committee member. It's the down-in-the-trenches lessons that they didn't teach in your college marketing courses. It's the stuff they don't cover at industry conferences.

If you're tasked with finding members for your club you will find instructions, best practices and little known hacks for building club membership in a sustainable way inside this book.

Whether you're just getting started or you're a seasoned pro, this will be your go to desktop companion when formulating your club's marketing strategy for many years to come.

Order at MembershipMarketingBook.com

The ABC's of Plutonium Private Club Leadership

Co-authored by Michael Crandal, CNG and featuring 16 private club experts from around the globe.

This isn't some boring textbook filled with academic knowledge. This is a seriously fun guide filled with real world, in-the-trenches leadership and management advice. We scoured the globe to find the top minds in private club leadership and management and compiled their advice in this fascinating easy-to-read guide.

Order at http://plutonium.club

Moving Targets: Creating Engaging Brands in an On-Demand World

Moving Targets is a guidebook for creating and re-inventing brands in today's on-demand world. Our culture, and consequently our marketplace, has become faster and more impersonal. Great brands have adapted by increasing their speed of delivery and learning to connect with consumers on an intimate, more emotional level.

This book will teach you how to build a sustainable brand that captures a loyal customer base for your product or service. Weaving fundamental branding concepts, personal anecdotes and interviews with top executives, "Moving Targets" will help you leverage the wisdom of the top brands and apply it practically in your business.

Order at bit.ly/on-amazon

Notes

Notes

Notes

Notes

Notes

THE PRIVATECLUB AGENCY

THE PRIVATECLUB AGENCY

www.ingramcontent.com/pod-product-compliance
Lightning Source LLC
Chambersburg PA
CBHW031931090426
42811CB00002B/150